WARREN

WARREN

Karina van Berkum

MADHAT PRESS
CHESHIRE, MASSACHUSETTS

MadHat Press
MadHat Incorporated
PO Box 422, Cheshire, MA 01225

The Library of Congress has assigned
this edition a Control Number of
2021945506

ISBN 978-1-952335-31-0 (paperback)

Text by Karina van Berkum
Author photo by Keara Ziegerer
Book design MadHat Press
Cover image: *The Warren*, copyright © 2013 Kat Philbin,
8"x10" ink and watercolor on paper

www.madhat-press.com

First Printing

Printed in the United States of America

To my parents

Table of Contents

I.

II.

III.

VI.

VII.

I.

No Earthquake

Your town moves mid-dream, staggering
The china. The yard seizes up
Its collection of roots

Who will later die patiently
Into those long pores
They're leaving.

In the clamor you begin
To understand Spring, who has
Always scratched from the inside

Out of her young body.
You never heard her wildness,
Then such a static little secret and now

The freight train at the door.
Maybe you should have listened closer
But you are so human. You are afraid

Of greatness and cannot know
This shaking is nothing
But real need to bloom.

Herd

Facts make the droves of buffalo that used to slip
By me—bent with half-sleep—seem less
Wonderful. Silly facts, ruthlessly quantifying
The dark herd swallowing past our hatchback
Into Wyoming's wild throat.

When I first heard the term *Quantum Entanglement*
I smiled. I was ten, all elbows and an open face, in love
With the way sounds felt: Quanment. Entangletum.
Enquamgletang! Lement. Lament. Ment. Meant.
Einstein called it *spooky action at a distance.*

I imagined a bouquet becoming a crow,
Contagious witchcraft, though facts
Say it is neither. Quantum Entanglement
Refers to *a mass of particles scientists try*
To extract and recognize independently.

Doing this matters, probably. These are the facts.
Untangling particles means a lot
To someone who is not a child
In the backseat, whispering *lament*
At a herd's smearing silhouette.

"Pass the Red Spray Paint"

Red, the hard smell of a new calf
In Holland.

Red, a bite
Into hot fruit.

Red, the shape of my father's mouth
On the phone at the counter

And his carriage under Oma's
Hospital lights—
Silent. Living.

I was the one
At the doorway
With no epiphany

Like a suspended trout
Who never wanted

That red,
Dancing worm.

Warren

When you wake up slow, even at eleven
Years old, morning does too—it covers you
In the weird hours when Ma's gone already, deep
Into another breakfast shift or something. Though
You feel even more alone than that; it's hard to explain.
There are six dollar bills on the counter.

So you get hypnotic at the Saturday shows.
Spread dead center on the fourth-hand futon,
Left by sister who grew up
Forever ago. Rabbits do this too, kid,
You know. They wake and scan the warren
With the same glass-eyed caution, already understanding

That breakfast is somewhere out in the big world.
You're a rabbit in the morning, but it's not that easy,
Wisecrack you're half-watching now
On the crummy TV box, where Bugs has got
Your back, and will stay
Chased and wily, incredibly alive.

Hunting Scenes in Films

Make me feel all
Powerful. I watch
With happy hackles up as
The high-res furrowed man-brow
Cuts to red, close up
Stag distress. Another easy kill.

But if I really hitched a weapon
And mapped the estrus
Of local does, I would be wrecked
With worry. Not only
Have I never hunted, never
Negotiated a piqued trigger,

But how to proceed
Without movie magic? Without
That agonal close-up
That puts the eyes of
Simply everyone
Top of mind? Not just mine.

Will I know how sovereign to feel
Without it? Will I know I am
The man? I couldn't stomach
The big silence
After my gunfire went out—
The two flashing reports.

I Don't Know What to Love

Brothers toss shirts,
Become pink, become brown,
And I drown happy in the hot
Clatter of the place. I watch
The blue and pass the days.

We are camping.
Shake our towels and
Call them clean.
Father says little but
Desert meets sea.

On a crooked site on a hill
On this island I am moved
By the faraway boats
That slide along
Horizon's back.

Mother, every evening
Hanging wet suits sings
Through dimming light
Until behind her, like moons
They come.

I learn fast that they
Are the awful cruise ships
I've heard about.
Royal, Princess, Caribbean.
Slick with artifice,

Grubby dollar bills, plastered
Smiles on the trapped
Performers. For years
I've been reminded
Of their up-close ugliness.

But I watch now, helpless,
These crowns moving
Slowly toward their king, my god,
These jewels! By day they are nothing—blue
Against impossible blue.

Karina van Berkum

Girl Late in Spring

She is young, flower prodding,
Kicking homeward after a delivery.

Socks puddle over her shoes,
She chews her lips, arranges the place

Into careful little cairns. Bumbles
Over root knuckles while humming

The same scrap over and over
Of a tune. Doesn't even think

When squatting
To bother that fat

Scramble of a toad. God
Let's not tell her she's late.

"Does Your Family Have a History of Suicide?"

I fight with my family in exclusive silence.
Someone feels belittled. Someone's mad
Over a lolling career and brought it back
On his face, shadowy as a moor.

Someone is grieving her childhood
Again, face wet against the old dog who will soon
Be a photo like the others on the fridge.
Nobody lives that long and we know it.

We are silent only once on purpose: Christmas
Eve, with its colors on the ceiling and relative peace.
And me urging myself away from the thought:
Which of us will it be?

Pet

I am coiled kitty-corner to everything
In my one-room home. In these early

Mottled hours I am in and out of sleep,
Out when the rabbit noses my lip or cheek.

He is the center star of my crescent
Body, wants to be petted on his pied face

Which lowers with gratitude, clicking teeth.
I wonder if he understands sleep.

Mine or his own, which he must do
When the rest of the warren—me, my shadow

And his—are out. Maybe he thinks my affection
Keeps dying as I do, small mortems every morning.

His nudging is awe or annoyance.
Either he needs my touch as witness, or it is love.

II.

No Cartographer

Rivers riddle the map of a mind
Whose sickness, indiscernible
But wild, is riled.

The heart's map is another
Matter. Without the delicate N
Of orientation, it sprawls

Bright on big walls growing
Ranges labeled in languages
Nobody speaks.

The map of the eye is torn
And bare. It stares—stars
And borders unassigned

When unrolled
Like a scroll one more
Terrible time.

Staten Island

In college I spent six months lying
My way into friendships,
Then truthed them to death

And stood staring at the bodies
In lofted beds
Whispering about me.

In hot despair, I went to
The Staten Island Zoo, carefully
Selecting a compact disc to stir

In my angel-white Walkman.
It was early spring, 2008. The songs
Were haunted and the place

Was empty, full of brown rocks
In brown enclosures.
Maybe I was trespassing.

It rained. In a different version
Of this, animals appeared
From all sides to

Befriend me. But really
I saw only one tremendous
Cat in a cage.

Bright Red Birthmark

If my port-wine birthmark
Could sing, it would
Be operatic.

No, it is not feeling nor forlorn,
But looks loud
And peals out of me.

Trapped in my skin, the red
Vessels crowd—
The way salmon urge

Against a sudden and
Fattening net.
And while ugly,

My birthmark
Boasts a view: it is perched
High on the head, wedged

As if hastily
Between eye and hair-
Line (one dauntless brow

Spawning up and through),
Poised to notice
All the life I do.

And if it could
Trillingly narrate me,
I might not mind

Being mute. My voice
Would seem silly—who
Needs words if heady

Arias can sing what the
Heart hopes to say?
I saw a matinee

Once alone in some
European Staatsoper.
While pale sopranos'

Red mouths heaved
Unrequited love-
Lornities, I sat

And wondered how
My birthmark
Looked on me.

Who Is Living Here

Dogs pour through
The busted veins of Cusco Peru.

They come rotting and collect
Like an attic vase spilling

Sun-warmed dead wasps. The first
Torrents of life between waking

Fruit markets, the mutts will later
Clot up the roadside

While vendors call *Passion*
Fruit for sale, sweet papaya—cheap!

Plagues of dogs
Either wail or sleep.

Prague and Tongue

Like *Tongue,* the word
Prague is spelled
For its swollen center

And placement,
Which snakes before
It stalls.

This winter I hid inside
Both for a time
While the lead-faced

Neighbors worked fast
On their own
Obsessions. Alone

I learned to be in love
With neither town
Nor appendage

Whose shining, wasted
Forms ache against
One another:

Prague from Tongue
In a moment of silent
Lunacy, say,

And Tongue, sitting wet
In a gray station,
Dying to go.

Alone in Spring

Inside the clicking slither
Of this lowing bus

I breathe into near-Spring.
Watercolor buspeople bend

Like ribs and some graffiti
Shouts *Humana!*

While winter slips
From the city in secret.

I think an ooze of poetry
Must be creeping

In from the country,
Calling its sounds

Home like missing children.
This and recognition

Are the only desires
Of language.

But I'm on the 183,
Words swelling

To sentences in my ribs. And
The haunting of February's wet

Eulogy and the buds
Who will not wait.

The Windmills of Kinderdijk

That summer she wrote about the windmills
Dashing against her bus route. Twenty, reedy
And nearly soundless, she worked for Tante

As a stenographer an hour away.
Spent both ways scratching maudlin lines
Into an office pad in her lap. Using words like

Looming, elephantine, lord, the windmills
Felt important. Whatever they were
They were hers when she called them elephantine.

In August, a big one bent at the waist to embrace her.
She recoiled at the soft trouble of its touch:
Petal-limp, powerless—*The way a clean sky feels*

The weight of its light, she wrote. Then, shrinking
Back through the bus window as the mill stood,
She cried for it to be what it seemed.

The Whole Place Is Moondipped

From the grimiest barstool in the belly of a borough
You say this city is a river. I say it's a sea. You say no,
A river for its constancy, those slick coats
In a row and the daily *shoop* of dreams
Dipping into manholes. At least a river
Has direction, you say.

But my city is a point-less mass and
I am a big animal caught in it. The whole place
Is moondipped. I have learned to go with the swells—
Froth-topped, heady, heavy, heavying me. Trying
Not to sink looks like swimming but I am ready
For a wet hibernation, I say.

Karina van Berkum

The Residents of Narsaq

Ravens weigh
This vista down.
You see a hundred, two

At a time and they are
Always bluer than you think
They will be. See

Their heads rise
From ready breasts, kitschy foul,
As if the winter has dark teeth.

A Greenlander told me
The infant-sized ravens will keep
Punishing the rooftops,

Callusing their calls.
Casing the arctic—
Until they're done with us.

They fly low he said,
To remember
Your face.

III.

No Congregation

See the ivy,
Snarled and resigned,
Like the sleeping hands
Of a waking priest

Just inside.
He's off the clock, feeds
The finch, fingers
Pills and runs the rag.

Like his tired mind
The ivy sighs, tries
A lacerated little
At a time.

When He Saw She Was A Grown-Up He Gnashed His Little Pearls at Her

Is a quote from JM Barrie
Who wrote the book on my boy's
Biggest fear: the titular Peter.
My son thinks the nymph
Will squire him away to an ingrown fate
In a stump where he will be forced to share
Hammocks with strangers. *Think of this*
I said, *he flies. He might teach you.*
And Boy rolled his eyes and said
Mom that's fantasy.
I first read Barrie's pale-yellow
Peter book deeply unhappy
But young enough
To believe in fairies.
Young enough to believe in sons.

Mona

Mona mourns for Spring. At first cold she zhuzhes the master
Bedroom curtains closed and stays for days

Then weeks, her wallpaper is the landscape now, the sconces
Umbrellas where a little boy in shorts might sit with nanny.

Mona will not miss the begging tulips because they are here:
Ripe tissues sprouting from the bureau by the river. She grins

Just so. Waits until the rain lets up then spreads an old
Picnic blanket over this field, stained with Mona.

Mona this morning, Mona's last supper. Soon the robins
Are out; they rage against the mountainside. She kills one

With her hand and smears what's left on the bright lawn.
It is spring! Has been for years. There is dancing.

Someone is asleep in the river
And Mona creeps over him every time.

Karina van Berkum

On Eggshells

Who would be an egg
Who could help it?
Weighted dizzy, all head,
And everyone baited
For your weird death
Any second.

Holding you is like the
Near-sleep body pitch—
The instant you know
You'll never
Be ready
Nor steady.

Dead Man's Switch

The trigger for the Dead Man's Switch is neglect: conductor's
Heart fails, so he lets go, signaling the train to slow,

Commuters gripe and some never know. The trigger
Is inaction: the sweaty red button finally free of the villain

Finger. Sometimes followed by a big blast but, more often,
Less ceremony. No frills—the train car shrugging to a stop.

Nothing, that's the key, as if the dead man's switch
Understands despondency and wants to do something about it.

Think of the perennial work of mother earth, to keep
Her buds on the up and up. If she keels, fists

The buds, tucks to take eternal rest, that's it—her sprawling
Neglect is the switch. And then, who knows, maybe bedlam.

Maybe all the world a silent white explosion. Maybe not.
Whoever set the dead man's switch decides, and sometimes

Commuters get to work on time. In Queens, a password
Guards a wheezy screen, a Dell, '04. Six digits

Remembered forever by Evelyn, who cleans houses. Her kids,
Now grown, and the ladies at the Y have always wondered.

She maybe just wanted something that was hers to hide.
Told them, *don't worry—you'll have the secret when I die.*

Morningtime

An hour I've watched the sun's eggy strands
Creep toward my clock and harry its hands.

A patient attack, like a neighborhood cat
Considering which moving morsel to bat.

Like lichen on which cragged branch to start forming—
Drunk on the spot on the tree it's adorning.

Like a silent disease, which new cell to infest,
Or limb to climb in and then sweetly digest.

Like two men waltzing while neither
Presume they're on fire

Inside the clock
In my room.

The Fantasy of Hans Christian Andersen

Ariel, belle of the sea, drunk on a bar stool next to me.
She grieves, says she feels suckered, did not sprout the legs

She was promised. A siren-red matte clings head to shoulders
As she sobs, *I am not a woman and I am not a fish*. A murky

Gin, her third, gestures in her lily-knuckled grip. I think,
What a dreamer. Who could help but adore such a creature?

I read once that the Danish novelist who imagined her
Was celibate. His hidden journal said, MY BLOOD

WANTS LOVE. I pity big-eyed Ariel, now draping wet over
The marble belly of the bar; she is the candied contortion

Of his original lust. When she looks up her teardrops are severe.
They cut tracks, so when I see one start from her mouth I know

It is blood. I stun, follow their ooze to a pool on the blue rubber
Floor 'round a pile of her salty insides. I had not noticed her

Missing lower half! All this time a mere torso propped
On the stool, snug in its seashell brassiere. With each weeping

Heave she has pumped from the place where her waist was
Severed a sludge of lungs, stomach, and parts of her heart.

The gin, too, must be mixed in. I now recall Andersen's entry:
MY BLOOD WANTS LOVE AS MY HEART DOES.

Like little Karen in his later fairy tale, whose possessed
Red shoes forced her to dance forever,

Ariel was misled. She misread.
Signed for a human soul, not legs.

Roach

He is instinctively grim.
Even the name makes brown

Scattering sounds.
Though Roach's true horror

Is in his failures: to break,
And later to simply right

Himself, flip his warm
Skyward belly back

To the world's fastening.
When I lie helpless like that

I am easily roused
By a hand or a clock's hand

Or my own moaning longevity.
Only Roach keeps

Still to die, and only he
Knows why.

Mountain Echo

To the baby, it is sound and shape, the face
Of his mother.

To his mother, it is for him.

To the hunted, it's death's
Quickening pulse.

In the morning, it's the first aperture.

To the scientist, it is a chaste ricochet.

To the dog, it is direction.

For the dreaming, it is color
Let out of a cage.

To the ranger, it's a heartbeat
With a mother.

To the percussionist, it is
A heartbeat's mother.

To the mourning,
It is mourning.

To the river, it is another
Lullaby.

To the old man
In bed, it dies
Again again dies
Again.

To the maidenhair fern, it is
An irrelevant nudge.

He Named Himself

Lyrebird, rumpled Australian ground fowl. He sings
The song of a gas-powered chainsaw. He hears it every time

A pink-cheeked forester cuts a flank of landscape
Then mimics the brattle until it syncs.

He named himself to lie, clacks and ticks like the strappy
Gear of a bird watching troupe. The men startle

And disorient as Lyrebird changes. He is now a thrush.
Later, a car alarm. This one is good for causing scatter.

He named himself because he knows his throat is different.
The tail too, its furies of feathers up behind, catching grime

Like a flue. His larynx is a syrinx; controlled like a tugged
Marionette harmonizing with itself. His throat lets him be

A thrush to a thrush. He named himself when scientists
Could not. Was he a pheasant? Partridge? Some grubby

Junglefowl brother? They couldn't name him then
And cannot find him now. He is lying bitter and hidden

All over the Illawarra, mocking the clamor of his home.
He feels smug inside his name but smug birds

Are still birds. He lies without concept of the words
He calls himself Liar—Lyrebird—but cannot know

As he nurses the drag of a chainsaw's song
That his name is a small stringed yoke, made to strum.

IV.

You Said, "Write a Poem for Me Baby"

I want to chew your heart like a plum,
Its pit. I want to—need it.

I want to kick your pointless
Collage projects off a cliff.

I want to be like you or, next best, to nest
In you like a Russian Doll. I want you

To be full of me again—to monopolize
Me, just inside, asleep

Against your spine and pride.
I want the dog back—he prefers me.

I want to hold your neck like a hungry noose.
Will you cry if I do? I want you to

So I can comfort you.
I want to burn the forest where we once lived

Together—if my heart is barren, my land
Should be too. I wish it were not Dad

Who named me, Mother, I want to know
What word I am to you.

Take

Hell, take anything and see
What happens. Take the hand
Of a traveler and she'll
Become stone, no longer
Free or alone. Take the feral shine
Of childhood from the kiddies
And watch them waste
Into their paper birthday plates
A man said
Take my love
To his lover and they both
Became blind
And their cats and geraniums died.

No Waterfront

Consider the sea is subtle
From a third floor
View. Go higher,

Beyond the dizzy tree line
Or that rotating restaurant
From your birthday.

From there the sea is
As big and arresting as you
Feel inside it, now

Thrash and kick all you want
Before leaning hopelessly in
To the subtle black surface.

I Leave Home

And rise with the gibbous
Moon and drive.
It leans peaceful like an unwatched breast.
I can just see it through the summer forest
There—there—there—there
And balk against such
A gentle anchor. Who to howl to?
Who could be mad at the moon?
I burn
Lovesick and young
Up the highway.

The Circle Game

Every morning there's a halo
Hanging from the corner
Of my girlfriend's four-post bed.
When she wakes, she picks it up,
Frames her face in it and cheeses for me.
I am in her witchcraft.
When the thing clatters to the ground
It feels like a lesson learned
For holding onto something like that.

Obsession

I do not bend, the way I imagine

A ligament might. In the mornings,

In the evenings, I go through the hour

Over hour carnival

Of excavating bones

From my soul's old anatomy.

A Use for the Padlock

Sunday hums and you're thinking
About jumping—the grinning need
To do it. The yellow-blue noon is nothing
To you, and you won't walk near the window

To make tea or beat the heat. The call, l'appel,
L'appel du vide. The phrase that means
A craving to leap sixteen
Stories to the 300 block of Cathedral Street

Does not fit in your American mouth.
And if it did, it would jump right out.
L'appel du vide, the void is on the line.
And the worst will come; tonight

You'll lock your ankle to the bed
To stop the simple wonders you seek
Even in sleep. You wonder, for the French,
If the call is as splendid when it speaks.

V.

Language and Love Are the Same

I was thrilled when John said there was a German word
That bunches, accordion-like, the sentiment of wanting

To die before the beloved. *Ya'aburnee: You bury me.*
And though he insisted, it did not seem German—

No marble-mouthed vowel droughts or consonant flocks—
But I pardoned what it seemed. I imagined Ya'aburnee

Seeable, smile-shaped, the smile bursting up her face,
Spilling down the street, into everybody's shoes and

Her one wilted pocket. The smile that keeps her too-big teeth
And came with me to the Striezelmarkt.

A smile like that might, too, be some kind of translation,
But Ya'aburnee is not Deutsch after all.

John was misinformed, misinformed me. It is Arabic
And cannot match the broken waltz of my beloved's

German tongue. You bury me, I want to say
In any language. I need her understanding.

Laura de Noves

The name is beloved.
When I learned of her chaste,
Petrarchan refusal
I had to have her. What kind
Of woman has the self-
Preservation to hide
Feelings forever
For the sake of art?
Of herself in art? Of some
Coy immortalization?
His name heads the lines
But her head is the lines.
See its dark
Crescent in the heart-
Sick spine?

Rachel

She was an elementary
School recess monitor,
Statuesque, every day the same.

Whorls of little hands
And voice bursts bobbed
Up and around her

Until she was covered and
Wonderfully unmoved.
From a field's distance

I watched Rachel's black hair.
It must have been
So obvious.

Late autumn lapped
The red ends of my scarf
And I could not help myself.

The Atheist's Girlfriend

Every morning there's a halo hanging
From the corner of my girlfriend's four post bed.
But god, it's tired. Its rim aches downward
Like Dali's soggy clocks while the true
Clock makes time with rhythm nearby.

When she wakes, my girlfriend will hold
The thing against her chest as if it's the last scrap
Of an unbelievable shroud. She will say
Things to it, prayers. I only know this

Because once I saw
Her ruined face
As she held on. She had forgotten
To send me home.

Sarah

You are different from my other lovers.
Soft and milk-faced, gentle scented, you
Are a long moony reflection

On the Dursey Sound.
I am caught in your nearness—
Nearer than the ivy to the wall is

I croon, and you ask for more
And more. Your hands hold me
Like a drippy, cut-out heart.

Karina van Berkum

No Midnight

You're overseas for two
Terrible winter weeks.
Our love is new and the space
Is alive between us. I wish the
World were not so spread.

I want the barren weight of you
At New Year's moment—
Seven, my time—where you must
Be reveling with me
At least in mind.

Lover

If I was truly wild
As you say
My mouth would burn
Others' to foreshadow
The hurt I'll do

Or I'd glow
Like so many
Northern lights.
Celestial green warning.

But my type of wild
Is cherry and the taste
Is slight

Like a pear slice
That met an olive once.

Sophie

Is walking towards me,
Her bird hands making plans
In their pockets. How like her
To wear a peacoat like that, to be cherry
Blonde still, after years, I'm unmovable

As she comes. I brace for her hurt
But Sophie shines
That smile across the
Enormous space
And I know I am mid-dream.

I think out
About the way my sleeping body
Must look: twisted socks
And the brutal face of
Old love as it
Preserves her.

From Laura

Who said anything
About hiding?
Do not forget my love

Is preserved with his,
My name more
Frequent by far.

Am I not still heaving
Down the husk
Of his dead pen?

That ink, which
Lived and dried
By me?

Karina van Berkum

Other Fish

My lust has grown
Up beautifully. It started
On rocks and docks
As polyps and now

Lumbers in the places
She might live. Every day
Scanning faces
Underwater.

If I Saw You Now

I used to picture us
Heart-stopped in some crosswalk
Some Sunday. Or you showing up like snowfall

On my deck with your face and that one
Vest, ready to love me. An opera peals
From us, I think.

Now I picture me
Being honest at you from across the same
Indifferent street. My face

Explaining itself, my mouth
A frozen bud, and the now
Seasons between us pendent.

You'll walk away again
But on my watch, holding
The hurt you made like a clay animal.

VI.

Becoming Twins

Every night my children
Work hard to become twins.
They seem to nearly congeal,
Put rocks in each other's
Little shoes to match limps,
Share an orange—four and a half
Bright wedges each.

If they could they'd stitch
Themselves together.
Real needles, real thread.
I had to laugh when they asked
Permission. The blood
On our Animal Babies carpet
Would happily combine.

When I wake up childless,
Am I relieved? Am I one
Of them? Who would be
A mother who could help it?
I eat my own
Ten drippy wedges,
Ruined for love.

Karina van Berkum

Logan at Five Begins

Every story with a warning:
And you won't believe it—

As if that must be true.
As if he knows the old

Trouble of my heart's dis
Ease or

The dangers of dismissing
Some inevitable wonder.

Logan at last
Reaches the end

Of his drifting anecdote.
It is about the colors of a bug

He saw, the words up
And out his Cheshire mouth

Like the haunt of new
Life his sad mother

Five years ago
Simply could not believe.

Die

We play one 20-sided die
Whose bright faces

And delicate 0s are cut so
Small I squint at the stop site.

I skim the thing like a stone and lose it
Beneath the sink or the dog

Who wishes I wouldn't.
My opponent is six. He cares

About the numbers. Calls them out
Competition-style—our new record!

But I am tired of flying
Shapes, their odd ends.

I'd rather have a die
Without sides, without weight.

Karina van Berkum

I Want What She Has

My mother seems the combined
Narrative of those who have passed
Through her peaceably, then wrecked
Around as she raised them.
She dresses red and purple and

Her worry is just as bright.
I want to say I miss
Who she was before
We were born. Did I say I want her
Off a cliff? I only meant

The parts that are not her, the scraps
From her latest project, the Stuffed Animal
Hall of Fame. The too-heavy earrings
Can stay if only
As a knobby gold rope

That I will climb like a prince.
At the summit, I'll whisper about
These blisters she made. She makes
Such a beautiful fuss about motherhood
As though it has anything to do with me.

The Barren Wife's Monologue

I imagine my sons pushing up through the soil
In a row on a lowland plot. Imagine them rising
Like peonies but
Wretchedly human, coming up
Twisting and wet. And they look
Like me: hard-eyed. A chin dimple on one
Late bloomer. And they need me so
I mind the plot, weed a circle
Around the fattening knees.

After some years I imagine
The place spangled with my cowlicked kids.
Ten hardy rows or a dozen hollering
And knocking heads.
I bring water, I check on them but in autumn they die.
No exceptions—each body buckles back
Into the country, richening the peat. And my heart
Stays secret and the weeds erupt
Without ceremony or space for a grave.

Bird Watching

Albatross with winged eyes and careful fades
And ancient pride waits for one new
Albatross on an edge of angry sea.
She cries horribly
As I sidle up to her egg
To show my still-swollen middle
Where mine shrank back to sleep on me.

VII.

Musical Theater

I've started listening to *Jesus Christ*
Superstar and it feeds me the way
Church used to

When I broke in
Midday, open anyway,
And stalked the naves.

I've never heard a real
Sermon but it felt like music
When my footfalls resounded

And dust twisted up
Like belief, a response.
What else is that empty?

Now the big wooden doors
Are locked and I
Have stopped trying.

I cradle my atheism
And call folks Bible Thumpers
So they'll never get me.

But I fall back
On the lyric *He scares me so*
When he does.

The Morning Of

This morning the light's
Rhombus rays are knife
Tossed into my home.

The sink clicks and I know
If something horrible happens
Later on, I will keep these particulars.

I will fast preserve all that I am,
Even now, readying to forget.
The light knives will be brilliant

And so much bigger.
The dripping faucet will finally
Have its hooks in me.

Allegro

You've started ageing aloud.
Is it a big cartoonish tick-
Tocking or the slaps of closing
In steps? Or less metronomic,
A balloon's wet falsetto? In-
Or exhaling,
No way to tell.
The courier has never stopped knocking.
The quiet counting of the children you've forgotten
To pick up. The loud bleeding of the stream.

No Dreaming

Help me mine my sleep, my love.
Should I write what I have seen?

The Atheist's Pet

The rabbit died because I finally asked
Them to kill it.
Euthanasia for the body only

Please, let's see
Where the soul ends up—
I'd never even wondered

Before at sixteen or thirty
Because I had never
Held something so dead

Against my long living
Barrel of a body.
For one half breath

I wished it was me,
Then took it back fast
From whatever I was

Suddenly believing in—
What if it accepts
Only requests for death?

No Haunting

I stand tall
In a tight copse in the forest
I admit slipped my mind.

Living must be
A deconstruction of the slow-souled
Child who stood in for you

Or who you stand crookedly
In for now. Don't you understand?
There's been a death.

These warrened firs breathe more
Quickly now that there
Is somewhere to be.

Sixteen Years

The last time I flew I noticed
Myself in the assigned looking glass
Of 24B. It was me at sixteen,
Sixteen years ago. She spilled coffee,
Ate old almonds from the cavern
Of the carry-on. We smiled shyly
At one another.

Have I grown into or out of her?
Have I retracted her gangly arms,
Mirror glances, and will-be lost rings?
Can I right myself now, civilly
Secure my coffee lid? I am still
So afraid of crookedness,
Or heaven forbid a spill.

Acknowledgments

Thank you, D. Eric Parkison, for being my second pair of eyes on this book, as well as Kevin Gallagher and Marc Vincenz for your professional and creative encouragement. Thank you Mom and Dad, Nunu, Cheryl Asselin, Alice and the Corners, Liza, Cait, Christa, and Matt Kubacki for your continued love and support. And thank you to my brothers, Ben and Jake, for simply everything.

"I Leave Home" previously appeared in *Five Points*.

"You Said, 'Write A Poem for Me Baby'" previously appeared in *Ploughshares*.

"The Barren Wife's Monologue'" previously appeared in *The American Journal of Poetry*.

"Bird Watching," "No Cartographer" and "The Whole Place is Moondipped" previously appeared in *Unlikely Stories*.

"Logan at Five Begins" previously appeared in *Woven Tales Press*.

"Take" and "If I Saw You Now" previously appeared in *Beltway Poetry Quarterly*.

"Other Fish" previously appeared in *Right Hand Pointing*.

About the Author

KARINA VAN BERKUM is an editor and poet. She grew up in rural New Hampshire and finds herself returning to the woods. She enjoys writing about family, childhood, queerness, animals, and the wonderful places she's traveled and worked, including Greenland, South Africa, Slovakia, Peru, and Austria. She was a 2016 Robert Pinsky Poetry Teaching Fellow at Boston University where she received the Hurley Prize in Poetry, and she has taught creative writing at GrubStreet and Boston University. Her work has appeared in publications such as *Ploughshares, Five Points, Unlikely Stories, Woven Tales Press, Beltway Poetry Quarterly, The American Journal of Poetry,* and *Strange Horizons,* for which she received a Rhysling Award nomination for outstanding poetry. Karina now lives in Vermont where she is the Editorial Project Coordinator for MIT Sloan Management Review and the co-editor of *SpoKe,* a poetry annual. *Warren* is her first book.